Wisdom of the Sower

Lawrence Muigai

Published by Lawrence Muigai, 2022.

While every precaution has been taken in the preparation of this book, the publisher assumes no responsibility for errors or omissions, or for damages resulting from the use of the information contained herein.

WISDOM OF THE SOWER

First edition. October 31, 2022.

ISBN: 979-8224371242

Written by Lawrence Muigai.

Table of Contents

Wisdom of The Sower 1

forward 2

Introduction 3

The Time to Start is Now 5

The Time to Start is Now 6

Be the Change You Want 14

It's Doable 21

It's Doable 22

Start Small, Think Big 26

Start Small, Think Big 27

Get as Much Help 36

Get as Much Help 37

Be Ready For Success 41

Be Ready For Success 42

Set Your Eyes on the Bigger Game 48

Set Your Eyes on the Bigger Game 49

There's room for Improvement 53

There's room for Improvement 54

Dedication

To my dearest brother,

In the depths of your struggles, I've witnessed your unwavering strength and resilience. Your journey, though fraught with challenges, has inspired me to embark on a quest of my own – to illuminate the path of hope amidst the shadows of despair.

This book is not just a collection of words; it's a testament to the boundless love I hold for you. As I watched you navigate life's tumultuous seas, I couldn't help but feel compelled to extend a lifeline of hope, crafted from the depths of my heart.

May these pages serve as a beacon of light during your darkest hours, guiding you towards a future filled with promise and possibility. Know that you are not alone in this journey; your courage and resilience have ignited a flame of inspiration within me, and I am eternally grateful for the opportunity to walk alongside you.

With every word penned, my love for you grows stronger, and my determination to see you rise above your circumstances burns brighter. Together, let us defy the odds and rewrite the narrative of your life, one chapter at a time.

Forever and always, your devoted sibling.

Wisdom of The Sower

Seeds of greatness

`Plant the seeds of happiness, hope, success and love; it will all come back to you in abundance. This is the law of nature- Steve Maraboli

Hope lies in dreams, in imagination, and in the courage of those who dare to make dreams into reality- Jonas Salk

forward

Sometimes we feel like we are lost, stranded, not knowing what to do. Sometimes we feel like giving up is even a choice, considering what life has thrown our way. We feel like giving life another chance is a far-fetched idea.

But here I share with you reasons and ways you should stand up again after every fall and fight. Here I show you how much more you are made up of and why you should get your hands dirtier and your resolve firmer.

Wisdom of the Sower is a book all about you being more motivated to take control of your life and doing the otherwise impossible. I hope to change your mind set by the end of your reading, if you are brave enough to put what you read into practice.

Introduction

There once lived in a certain village a man who had nothing except a sizeable piece of land. The villagers looked down on him because he had nothing to offer. No one could invite him to any occasion since he had nothing to offer except to eat, drink and hobble about poverty and the government in any gathering.

Then one day he decided to change his narrative. He was fed-up with being mistreated in public, isolated by others, being inconsequential. He wanted to make something out of his life. He wanted to make good of his life.

The man put all his weight into all he had, tilling his piece of land. It was quite challenging but told himself it was doable. Withing 10 days he had cleared and dug up half an acre of his land. He dug furrows and, with the little he'd collected from well-wishers, cultivated his land. He spent most of his time tending to his crop and the spare time on digging up extra portions of his land, however small. When he saw he was going to receive a bumper harvest, he cut trees from his land and erected a store house. He knew he had to be prepared for his produce.

The man had some difficulty harvesting all his produce alone but he managed. He chose the best of his produce and set it aside as seed for the next season, while storing the rest in his barn. It struck him that he could plant even before the next rain and immediately went to work. He'd already reclaimed another 2 acres of land by then, that had previously lain idle, so now he sowed a bigger piece of land than before. Some of the villagers made fun of him as he juggled between fetching water for his crop from a nearby river and digging a well in the middle of his land. Ha knew he had to do it so he turned a deaf ear to them.

His crop was in full flower by next rains. The man had food enough to last him for the next six months in his store house and enough seed to sow the rest of his farm. He sold some of what he had in the storehouse and employed young men to clear and dig up his idle lands. He had already tilled and sowed by next rains. He sold some of the trees the young men had cut down as firewood and used the straighter and sturdier ones to build a bigger storehouse. He was expecting a bigger harvest and would rather be prepared for it.

By and by, the man's idle land became a farm. His neighbours stopped calling him "the man" and started referring to him as "farmer". He frequently invited extension officers to his farm and acquired better farming practices. He leased lands from his neighbours and sowed in and out of season. People from far and wide flocked to his farm to seek advice, study smart farming or seek employment.

With time, the village beggar had turned to a farmer and finally a great investor.

The Time to Start is Now

The way to get started is to quit talking and begin doing – Walt Disney

The Time to Start is Now

Life is full of ups and downs. Some of us are born into rich families while others don't have the privilege. In this regard, most people are caught up in the defeatist mindset that they are not born in the well-to-do families so they won't soar as high. The truth of the matter is quite the opposite. The situation you were born in does not have to affect what you'll be, unless you allow it.

And who said you were born poor in the first place? In her song "Court of Many Colours", Dolly Parton says, "... one is only poor only if they choose to be." Because you slept on an empty stomach for more than enough nights does to mean your family was poor. Your parents were trying their best to give you the best in life. Was the whole of your family poor because your parents could not give you what others had? No.

Those people we regard as poor might have the best ideas that could change the world; a wealth of ideas, I might say. Our parents had a wealth of ideas, projects that one could start and grow wealthy in money.... but not them, not now. They kept postponing those ideas and projects waiting for something that ought to have happened. They held the poultry project off for until you joined nursery school. There was a problem because your new school uniform spent most of what they had saved up. They could put it off till next term when they'd have some cash, next year, next....... Thirty years later and the poultry project remains a dream.

What if they put their idea into practice, what if they injected a couple of chicks into the backyard every week? What if they swapped that kilo of meat for a couple of chicks? By the end of the year they'd have had more than a hundred chicken quacking around. But they didn't. They waited for until a time when they'd have enough capital to start. Like you, they waited for the opportune time. Like them, you are waiting for ABCDE to happen so you can do D.

Like those before us, we have wasted our time waiting for the next express train to take us there. The unfortunate thing is that the next express train is a long wait which may never end. Why not ditch the ride and be on the move? What you didn't realize is, you don't need the train as much as you need to get there. Start moving now. The journey to wherever you want to go starts where you are.

If you take the first step, the second, third and umpteenth will follow progressively. Your journey depends on continuous motion regardless of speed. These who have succeeded in life did so because they set in motion, stumbled, fell, got up again and resumed motion got a lift.... they realized that every journey starts with starting. They knew that life has no Uber where you can afford to get late waiting for a fast car to take you there on time. They didn't wait, they did!

The problem with waiting is that it requires you to wait. If you are patient enough you can wait forever. Though they say patience pays, it's an incomplete statement it only does so in rare occasions. These who are patient enough to do nothing about life, life does them. Don't wait f or life to do you coz it does not do good. If you are waiting for things for things to happen, know there are those who are snatching the good things out of life. Don't wait for things to happen, happen to things. Only go-getters get the good things out of life. You need to go out if you are going your desired things in life.

Don't think of life like a queue at a buffet where you are being pushed forward by those behind you to get your ration at the table. The simple fact is that there is no queue in life. Each one of us has their own destiny. We are not moving in the same direction even. Only you have the blueprint if not the map of your life's journey, so why wait for someone to tag you along? We all have different goals in life. You may think you have the same dream as may think you have the same dream as AMREF since you want to be a doctor, only to find that your goals, dreams and aspiration are as far as heaven and earth. Even in a football match the players of the same team don't have the same goal. One has the goal of scoring; another is a defender and another's goal is to prevent the opposite team from getting the ball into his net. Just when you thought you were playing towards the same goal with so-and-so, you realize you are in a different match altogether. The only thing we have in common is the universe as a common playground. Only you have a way of knowing when you have scored.

Only you can know when you have missed. Only you can decide if the game is over. In fact, only you can determine whether to kick off or not. If you get stuck in one place, if you don't play towards your goal, other players might tackle you inadvertently to the ground and there's no ref to give you a free kick. If you are waiting for life to employ a referee, you are in the wrong place. If you are waiting for success without undertaking something, not here. You can only succeed in doing something.

If you want to rise to greatness, then you must climb the ladder. Greatness does not happen; you must achieve it. you must try to see what happens. You must do something to see results. The only place that results come before trying is in the dictionary. You really must try to see what happens. The problem with so many people is that they keep thinking what will happen if they do this or that. What if what am thinking does not hold, does it have to, in the first place? What if things don't go according to plan, what if I don't succeed, what if I fail? By not trying something you are being a failure already.

Fear of failure is the greatest enemy to success. Many dreams have been killed by the fear of failure. Many potentially great men have wallowed in mediocrity for the fear of failure. They couldn't be brave enough to take the first step. Some remained there in the same position for the rest of their lives while others went back to what they knew better; a worse version of themselves. They failed to start, they failed to try, they failed in getting in the road to success, they failed to put their ideas into practice. If you fear failure, you have failed already.

You have failed so many times since birth that you can't remember, why fear one more failure? What difference would one more failure make to your life? As a new born you tried countless times to connect to your mother's breast and failed, till you overcame that challenge and succeeded. You failed in standing up and tried incessantly till you developed muscle enough to stand up and walk. You learnt how to speak, how to write through multiple failures. If you look back, you'll notice that your life's successes are made up of failures. You can't get to success unless you pass through failure. Don't let that mask of failure frighten you. If you fear so much, fear to remain where you are forever.

When Jesus from the Bible feared death from Herod, they got in the boat and crossed over to the other side. They'd rather risk storms in the sea than Herod. They knew they had a probability of surviving in the sea, of which they didn't have if they waited the king's soldiers to capture them. They used their fear of failure(death) to propel them on a journey to success (life. Don't let your fear keep you waiting for Herod. Don't wait for the storms to subside. In the storms of life there is a chance to shine through and be great. It's a pity they had to put 'failure 'way before 'success' in the dictionary, so you must get through failure before you can come to success.

So, I'm going to fail? Yes, countless times! You must fail your way to success. Someone tried many times to come up with these medications you like to take. Why else do you think animals were used to test the formulas first? These professionals, with their level of education, know that their formulas could fail but go ahead and concoct them anyway. Even after computer simulations in the lab they know they can't be 100% sure with their formulations. Yet they don't stop there. Their only way is to get started, try and modify along the way.

Don't wait till you are sure of success; you'll never be. Greatness starts when you take the risk. Your parents were not 100% sure you'll be born but they took the risk. They were not sure what you'd be spending for the next ten years after birth but they still took the risk. Had they decided to plan for your upkeep first, you'd probably be unborn even now. Planning was not in their mind, you were. What-ifs were not in their minds, you were. Your parents wanted you more than they'd care for your education, clothes and other basic amenities. They could always work out ways to give you the best once they have given birth to you.

That's one thing we could borrow from them. If a baby is more important than what they'd look like in 10 years then putting your idea into practice is more important than how it would work out. How many visitors will I be getting in my blog? Write your first bog post, the second, the third. Learn as you go. What will that lady say if I go talk to her? Approach her now and let the conversation flow. Where will I get customers for my bottled water? Package a few dozen bottles and get out into the street. Success starts with the first step.

If you take that first step now, you'll know where to put your foot next. Don't make the mistake of planning for the 100th step. You never know what you'll encounter along the way. Just get started. After all the only secret to getting there is getting started. No amount of planning will ever take you anywhere. Ok, they say, "If you fail to plan you plan to fail" but that's 2 failures already. If you plan and never do, you'll have wasted your time. You have planned enough all your life, start doing now. This is because the world is so dynamic, you'll ever find yourself planning for the changes it brings. The figures you planned with and for last month have since changed. The facts you planned with last year have changed. The solution is not to go back and plan again. Planning has already done as much harm to you. Your idea is collecting dust on the shelf because you are planning.

The big question is, do you accept your life to be a total failure because you chose to plan first? If procrastination is the thief of time, then planning is a hacker, if not an armed robber. It will hack your thinking and rob you of opportunities. Have you ever realized that many great things happen in your life without planning? Do you plan for your heartbeat, your breathing, how and to think? These are things that happen continuously and there's one thing that doesn't happen as continuously; do you plan for a fart? You just let it happen when it comes.

Don't hold back that fart. Don't hold back your ideas, they'll spoil your life if left inside you, the way air would your stomach. An idea in your head is nothing if not put into practice. You must put your ideas into practice if you want to rise to greatness. A multimillion plan will not add to your worth if you are not going to take the first step now. The problem with holding back ideas in the name of planning is that plans become obsolete with time. Don't get caught up in the habit of tweaking the outdated parts of your plan, get into the habit of moving with your ideas.

Before you, men died in mediocrity despite having great ideas. They also had dreams bigger than yours. They also had plans like yourself. They also envisioned a future that turned out to be a mirage. They were buried with a wealth of ideas, ideas that they held back in the name of planning. Don't make the mistake too. Don't die with your ideas while you can flourish now. You don't need to have the most brilliant ideas. You don't need to have the biggest outlay; you need to take action, now. The journey to greatness starts here and now. If you are going to do something, do it now. If you are going to start somewhere, start here. Don't wait for tomorrow coz it will be too late.

Don't wait to add wealth to the graveyard which is already affluent. Great ideas have been buried there in mediocre men. Only the land of the living needs your wealth of ideas. Don't wait till you are too old to dare. Do, now! Move your ideas the way you do air. Don't wait for people to say nice things or stop saying nasty things about you or your talents and ideas. After all people will talk anyway. Remember, the fear of failure is the beginning of mediocrity. Planning or not, do not hold back for another day. Start taking those baby steps now, for the journey to greatness starts here and now

Be the Change You Want

Some years ago, a woman friend of mine confided to me something she was going through. She had been married for 4 years with 1 child. Recently her husband evolved into a bully, beating her up every now and then. She had requested his parents to talk him out of it, only for matters to get worse. The husband started arriving home at ungodly hours, wearing a different perfume. If she dared to ask, that would be the beginning of another war.

The couple had gotten their first child in their first year of marriage. After the second year the man wanted another baby but nothing was forthcoming. For those two years the couple tried everything in their power to no avail. Now the man was demanding for the baby. The wife had suggested for both to be tested only for the man to bring his self-diagnosis results; he already had a son out of wedlock. The wife did the test alone and was found to be okay/ fertile. She was ready to forgive her husband's alluded extra-marital affair but the beatings! This woman confided to me when her husband mouthed to her something to the effect that even if he had to take the effect and be found impotent, that would mean that he was not the biological father of their only child and that would make things worse. Now here was my advice; if the kitchen gets too hot, get out.

We all have passed through such circumstances where we feel like we are pressed to the wall. It's natural to think we can hold on a bit longer and things will be okay, that things will change for the better. It always feels safer to remain in situations we are used to. It' perceived as comfortable not to agitate the waters as we trudge out, is it right? Is that what would give you optimal happiness in the long run? Is that what you'd choose if you could go back 10 or so years?

The devil you know can never be anywhere near as good as the angel you don't know. If you are bedding the devil and pretending, he's good, albeit at times, you know you're risking sucked at night. Knowing the devil doesn't make him any better. The devil remains the devil regardless of how much you are acquainted with him. A bad situation remains a bad situation. A dog's life remains a dog's life no matter how much you know how to survive. Mediocrity is mediocrity. If where you are is not where you dreamt of being, then you know you are not where you are supposed to be. You are in the wrong place: get out!

The problem with getting out of a situation you are used to is that you are leaving what you are used to for what you are not sure of. But the question remains, does getting used to that situation make it any better? Does getting used to a low-paying job make life any better. Does getting used to an abusive relationship make life easier?

There's a story of lepers who were put I a kind of isolation camp. Given the prevailing drought condition in the country the lepers were used to being under fed. They were used to being treated as less humans. They were use to being short-changed. That's the kind of life they were used to until one day, one of them came up with an idea; this was not the kind of life they wanted for themselves. They had regretted enough being lepers. They had blamed God enough for not healing them. They had cast their votes against the government more than enough times for stowing them away as if they were not human. As this man articulated his idea, he stomped his feet on the concrete floor, making sounds like those a f the hooves of a horse.

"eureka!", another leper shouted. The others looked at him as if he'd developed wings.

"What if we stomped our feet like this, all of us. What if we all leper made a beeline for the city!" The leper exclaimed to his comrades. They knew they'd die of hunger and starvation if they remained in the isolation camp so they decided to take the risk. They dared to break through the iron and mahogany doors. They dared to venture out. They dared to tear down the barricades. The sentinels would have only two options; to give us food or to kill us. They turned their fear into anger, anger born out of hunger, humiliation, mistreatment, lack and want.

The lepers stomped in near-unison towards the great city. When the soldiers heard the great noise approaching, they thought their city was under siege by a mighty army on horseback. The soldiers quickly shoved the king into a cargo wagon and the whole city fled. The lepers now had free unextruded access to the food banks. The previously malnourished lepers became food merchants overnight, selling supplies they'd plundered from the storehouses.

The lepers had lived in the bleak situation for as long as they thought the government was to blame, God was the problem, leprosy was the problem, the problem was the problem. But no one was their problem. You will remain stuck for as long as you don't realize anyone is your problem. Your greatest problem is not even the challenge itself but how you respond to it. If a lion is chasing you, you may decide to lie down flat or to climb a tree. Likewise, if there's a shoot-out you may decide to lie down flat or to climb a tree. The lion or the shoot-out is not the problem; the problem is you trying to climb a tree or stand in the middle of the street when there are bullets flying in the air.

Money, or lack thereof, is not your real problem. Nor is unemployment. Nor is capital. The relationship is not the problem, nor is your addiction. How you respond to the situation is what becomes the problem, or the solution. Quit blaming everyone for your situation. They already have theirs. Only you are responsible for your life. Quit trying to delegate that responsibility to others coz it can't be.

Quit waiting for the government to provide more employment opportunities. In fact, most governments are moving towards technological methods that require less workers. Don't blame your low pay on your company, you were not born there, so you can as well pack up. Don't blame your lack of capital on policy. Policy is stronger than you, you can't change how things have been operating. Instead of praying and trying to change how the world operates, change your thinking. Move from, "Hey, I'm a forgotten leper in an isolation camp, I am nothing" to, "I have to do something."

You may have wallowed in the notion that the world is unfair for so long, until now, that you realize that the world I as fair player. Life doesn't hurl challenges in your face and run. It gives you challenges to you to tackle with the tools you already have, and succeed. You only need a little creativity to connect the right tools with the challenge and exploit the opportunity in it. Did the lepers realize that being denied food was an investment opportunity, did they in their wildest dreams, in their more than 10 years, think that their leprosy-deformed feet would make for battle horses? It just started from their burning desire to live that they saw the flaws in the mahogany doors, heard done of them stomping like a horse and for the first time in history, knew there was food in the city.

It takes a burning desire to succeed for you to look at things from a different angle. Rarely will opportunities present themselves in a wedding gown with a banner that declares, "opportunity, just for you". Oftentimes you'll need to sweat off your pants through a challenge, step back, look from a different angle and see the opportunity side of it. No one ever said, "Come let us invent the wheel." It took the Egyptians some years of dragging loads of pumpkins on stretchers until a very tired man dropped his stretcher and the pumpkins rolled. They had trees that could make the wheel all the along. Yet they thought the pumpkins were the problem.

The situation itself is not the problem. The problem is you crying foul. Many have been there and seen the brighter side of it. Yet many, like you, have been there and looked at the darker side in the situation. That makes all the difference. The road to greatness starts when we refuse to see the problem in the opportunity and start taking positive action.

Many inventions were made to solve a certain problem. Before the invention was made there were many people who lived with the lack of something to perform ABCDE, and they continued to complain, like me and you. Then came someone who thought, "What if we wore hide under our feet?" before them men were getting blisters walking barefoot in the sand, until someone decided to look for a solution. If they complained about their blisters, they never got a viable solution, but the man who took his mind from the situation to the solution surely found it. Always set your eyes on the solution. Adam and Eve could have hidden forever since they were naked. But God made the first invention and clothed them in animal hide.

Don't make the mistake of hiding. There are times when we feel financially, socially, emotionally or otherwise naked. The most readily available option is to hide and complain. It is very easy to apportion blame and to complain but it doesn't solve anything. If blaming and complaining is all you are doing in the face of the situation you are helping nothing. You'll remain in the same situation for as long as you do nothing about it. Don't wait for the government to change. Don't wait for a miracle to happen. Don't wait for employment opportunities to present themselves.

If you wait for the world to do something for you, the world will do you and, mark you, the world does not know how to do good. No one else will change the situation for you; only you can. If you think that something needs to be changed, that's very good because only you can institute that change. Everyone else is busy dealing with their lives. Why would they be responsible for yours? Only you are responsible for your life. No one is responsible for your promotion, only you. Don't blame it on the next candidate. No one else is responsible for your investment, except you. No one else is responsible for your addiction. Just you. Your relationship, your employment or lack thereof, only you are answerable.

If you think of your life as your sole responsibility, then everything falls into perspective. You know for sure that only you can institute change. You know for sure who is responsible for your success or failure. You start thinking in the lines of what needs to be done not what the problem is. Just the way you are responsible for every transaction in your bank account, you are equally responsible for what goes on in your life. You can't choose what challenges life throws your way, but you can choose your reactions to these challenges. You can choose to turn those challenges to life-threatening problems or exploit them and succeed in life. Realize challenges for what they are, opportunities in disguise. Exploit them. Be the change you so much desire.

It's Doable

All our dreams can come true if we have the courage to pursue them-Walt Disney

It's Doable

There's this character I the Bible who saw Jesus walking on water and thought he could also walk on water. He walked on the surface of the sea for some moments till he thought like the sailor he was, "I can swim, but walking on water, who does that?" the moment he started thinking negatively about walking on water, he started sinking. He was succeeding till the moment he thought that what he was doing was impossible.

That's the greatest crime our minds commit against us. Like Peter, we are thinking of the logic of impossibility. You look at the circumstances and think how this is going to be a failure. You look at the economy and think you know that this is a bad time for business. You listen to a few people and think it's a bad idea to vie for elections. You look kat your past and think you are doomed. Your logical thinking doesn't always have to be right.

Just because someone tried and failed does not mean everyone will fail. Just because you failed a few times does not mean you are a total failure. Just because the figures don't look as good does not mean the whole project will not pull through. It just means, done in a traditional way, the project will go down, but not with a little creativity from you. It just means a particular doctor thinks you are doomed.

But it's not the gospel truth. You can always look for another one till you get the desired effect. Look for different methods to look at different circumstances from different angles. Have a little more creativity. Make that difference. The difference between the great and the average is that the average thinks normally. For you to attain greatness you must think out of the normal. Normal people would not entertain 76 lines of thought about an abstract thing like electricity. Normal people would not jump out of the faucet, look at the new water level, get back in again and, Eureka!

Great men are just like me and you, only they are crazy enough to think differently. If you want to join their league, you must embrace a different mindset. A can-do mindset. You must believe that everything you set your mind on can be done, and find ways to do it. If you can think it, you can do it.

How much you believe in your idea will translate to how you act. If y oar ensure you are doing the right thing then you'll put all your weight behind it. On the other hand, if you are doubtful of success you will employ a half-hearted effort and fail in the end. You fail, not because you don't have the right tools but because you have the wrong mindset. The mindset of failure. You fail to start something, not because you don't have the wherewithal, but because of doubt. If you are so good in doubting, you are good in failing. Don't allow doubt to hold you back. Great men start by believing in themselves.

Stop looking at the reasons why you can't float. Concentrate on the reasons why you should float. How you will float. Logic says Peter can't float in business. Logic says Peter can't float on politics. Logic says peter can't float with is grades. He knows he must float to stay alive. He knows there is a solution in the Name of Jesus and extends his hand. The moment he distracts his mind from the logic of sinking to the solution, he starts floating back to the surface.

Someone might have the solution. Ask for it. The problem with many people is that they suffer in silence while someone might be more than willing to offer help. Some people look at the possibility that others might laugh at them, make fun of them, refuse them help, spread rumours about them.... but it's better to ask for help and succeed than to suffer in silence. People will always have something to say behind your back. If they want to take credit for your success, let them have it. It's way better than to have them talk about your failure.

Don't hesitate to exploit that input you think could be in the other person. If they have what you want, go get it! If your undertaking needs outside help, don't sit back and do nothing about it. Do or be done. People always want to be associated with the great. Be that great person and let them flock around you. They can only know you have a great idea if you prove to them that it's doable.

All that the world is watching out for is your enthusiasm. People smell doubt and fear from a mile away. Don't let these feelings prey on you. Don't entertain them in your mind. Don't let doubt stand in the way of your success. Don't let fear make you doubt the ideas in your mind. If you can conceive that idea, be sure that it's viable. Have the faith of a fast-food dealer.

A fast-food dealer wakes up every morning, prepares his array of dishes and waits I perfect faith that customers will come to his kiosk and buy all of it. He doesn't worry about people not being hungry that day. He can't entertain the thought that people might be out of town that day. He doesn't entertain or harbor doubts that his food might go bad and attract him loss. He just prepares and waits.

Like the fast-food dealer, prepare and wait. Play your part and pray for the best. How else can you succeed without trying, who else will make it happen if it's not you? How will you make it if you don't believe in it? If your idea sounds crazy, be crazy enough to practice it. If the project sounds commonplace, start small. If it looks hard, who said everything should be easy. Grow a tough bone and face it off. You must be tough to get going.

No one has ever started something without ever encountering challenges. They had to get the ball rolling, ram into challenges, overcome them until they succeeded. What if they diverted their attention from the goal of the challenge? What if they only looked at the handicaps and never dared to look beyond? They'd never have succeeded. Success only happens to those who look beyond the challenges and overcome them.

If only you can dare to look beyond those challenges, if you can focus on your goals and let noting derail you. If only you could treat those drawbacks as setups for success. Then your life will be a success. You start implementing those ideas with a success mindset. You use that energy that you could have used to complain, to succeed. If only you could ditch those dark goggles for night vision. If only you could look from a different angle and realize how doable it is.

Start Small, Think Big

Start small, think big. Don't worry about too many things at once. Take a handful of simple things to begin with, and then progress to more complex things- Steve Jobs.

Start Small, Think Big

Many years ago, as a little boy, I got a life-changing lesson from my neighbour's son, who was I his mid-20s by then. It was a particularly hot afternoon and both of us were basking in the shade of a lone tree. After a long pause in our conversation he told me, "climb this tree from the top." I looked at him with confusion, which he rewarded by slapping a thousand-shilling-note on the ground, promising it would be mine if I managed to climb the tree from the top.

As a young, intelligent and creative boy, I tried all ways possible. I tried to use a nearby tree to sling myself onto the tree's top. I ended up hurting myself. I tried to pole-jump as they do in movies and failed painfully. I tried other creative methods and finally gave up tired ad paining. Still paining and dog-tired, I dejectedly came to sit beside him and the currency note, which I never earned (by the way a thousand shillings was a lot of money then). After laughing at me for a long time he told me something that stuck to my mind; you must start at the bottom.

Like me (younger me), many are trying to pole-jump to the top and even engaging their creative mind on the prospect of getting there without climbing up. That would be great if it could be done. All of us would be at the top. The sky would stop being the limit and there'd be no greater men coz all of us would be at that great level.

But we have a good problem here; you must start from the bottom. If you are not ready to climb up, successively putting on foot higher, you are not getting to the top sooner or later. You need to move up progressively from the base, otherwise you are going to hurt yourself and fail. You must be humble enough to accept where you are.

A great journey starts where you are not where you want to be. If you want to get there then you must have a clear appraisal of where you are. This is important for you to get your bearings and to know for sure which direction you want to take. Otherwise you'll be lost. Many people fail in life because they don't appraise and accept their current situation. They live in denial, creating a world around themselves, where they simply don't belong. Their imagined status makes them feel better but it doesn't make them any better.

If you want to make your life better you must accept your present status. You must look objectively at the facts and figures and know the kind of lifestyle you can afford now. Consider your health reports and know what you need to cut back on and what you must do now. It's looking at and executing life in a disciplined manner. Don't create an imaginary world around yourself, effectively lying to yourself. Know the real you. That imaginary you are unsustainable. He will keep sucking the life out of you, your health, your finances, your relationships.

If you are at the bottom, accept that as a fact. It's something you can change. You can't change your imaginary self. He will on be lying to you, making you feel good about yourself till you degenerate and die a poor man. It's time you climbed off your high horse and looked at things from natural perspective. Know what you can afford and what you cannot. Know where you can scratch and where you can't. know what you have and what you need.

After analysing yourself and knowing your true status, you'll be able to change things. You'll be ready for change. Only then can you see the holes that you can plug. Only then can you see the gaps that need to be filled. Only after removing the fancy cover can you see the flaws in your character, the deficits in your monthly budget, the needs that need to be addressed. You will have taken the first step towards greatness without realizing it, if you dare to know your true steps.

Self-appraisal is great, but don't get stuck there. Knowing your true self is like a doctor's diagnosis. It will only be helpful if you take those meds or go for therapy. Here again, taking all those pills in one go will not cure you overnight. They will kill you. You must take them one at its own time. Healing starts with the first pill. Don't make the mistake of taking your life's pills in one sitting; they'll destroy you. That's one thing that success has in common with healing. Just like healing, success is not sudden but a gradual process. You must be patient enough to progressively progress in your success path. Note that progress is never too swift, neither too slow but gradual.

Don't stumble over yourself trying to make 10 steps at a time. You'll hurt yourself. Instead, take one step in time. You only need one more step to get nearer to your desired goal. The problem with a great leap, as it were, is that you might sprain or break your leg. Why hurt yourself when there's a better way of doing things. Just take that one step and you'll be nearer to your goal.

The problem with most people is that they get stuck as they wait to leap over 16 steps and break into a run. That's how great dreams die a natural death. Don't join the bandwagon. Instead take the slow but sure route. Know that every step you take takes you closer. Focus on that one step. don't break into a run. Instead of waiting for that financial slingshot, start doing something small. Instead of waiting for a sponsor to pole-jump you, engage your muscles in taking successive steps.

The adage holds true that a great journey starts with a single step. That simple step you take is the one that makes all the difference, not your planning and preparation for the journey. Regardless of the distance or the greatness of the destination itself, those small steps make all the difference. No matter what your financial goals, political, social or intellectual goals look like, those small things you do make all the difference. If you don't take that simple step, you'll remain in the same position indefinitely.

The problem with most people is that they want to start multi-million projects all at once. if you ask people around, you'll be surprised with the great ideas they have. Projects that could rake in zillions of monies, character changes that could make them better people and improve their social life, courses they could take and land better jobs, political positions they envy. These people will tell you that their greatest problem is lack of where-with-all, but it can't be further than the truth. The only biggest thing between you and your dreams is those small baby steps, or lack thereof.

Sew that one stitch instead of waiting for nine. that's what they say, "A stitch in time saves nine". Taking one small step is more sensible than waiting to take very many leaps later, we are never sure of which time. You don't have to do something grand to be great and successful. it's okay if we all love grandiose but you do not want to be a slave of it. The way o wisdom is to work with what you have as you progressively acquire more. mark you, you don't need more than will-power to kickstart your journey to success.

The greatest scientists didn't have a lab to work in, they contented themselves with working from the kitchen. But look at science today, it has been shaped by those men who didn't have the apparatus we have today but worked with common household items to carry out their experiments. They refused to see the handicaps and used all that was available to them to make one of the most prolific and outstanding inventions.

If those scientists believed they were equipped to fulfil their dreams, you are better equipped now. You have access to more information, are exposed to better technology and have easier access to the larger world. You just need to leverage on those things that are available to you. There are farmers who produced ad transported their produce before the wheel. There are traders who transacted before money was invented. politics started and thrived way before PA systems were invented and developed. That set of tools you think you can't start without is to as great as your dreams. It's not even half-way as important.

Instead of wasting your time, brain and resources looking for those implements, start off with or without, and let them find you along the way. Men have succeeded in life after starting off as hawkers. We have seen bottled water companies bloom out from hawkers who started by selling water in plastic bags on the streets. Large chain supermarkets have been born out of commonplace kiosks. Why wait till 2098 to start your multi-billion projects while you are now in the range of hundreds and thousands? Start something small and grow with it as you go. That is the natural flow of life.

If you look back at the most basic things in life, you'll be surprised that you can draw a lot of wisdom from them. The greatest speakers didn't know how to utter a word when they were born, just like you and me. Slowly they learnt to pronounce 'papa", form a few crooked sentences, request for their favourite toy, till one day mama told them to thank a visitor for one thing or the other. Some of them were even shy to recite memory verses in church school but by and by they learnt to speak in public and move crowds.

The greatest athletes were born with weak bones and muscles like me and you. slowly they learnt to sit up, crawl, to prop up un objects. They took their first steps and fell, just like you and me. they trotted and stumbled on themselves. like you and me. They gradually developed their muscles by running errands, like all of us, and doing ordinary jobs. They discovered they could use their muscles to a greater advantage and went an extra mile to develop them even more. By and by, common people with common limbs like you and I developed what they had and propelled themselves to greatness.

Look at writers; they have the same hands we have. We wrote the same essays in school. Singers have the same voice-cords we have. Athletes have the same set of limbs. All of them were performing the same tasks as we, with the same body parts until they decided to exploit them further. They didn't acquire a new set of limbs, ears or voice cords. They started with what they already had and what they had adjusted to their new demands. Neither did they succeed overnight, the singers kept at it till their vocals developed beyond oscar quality. They kept at it till their bodies adjusted and perfected to the new success-demanding climate. They suffered blows, ran to 16th position in local arenas till they developed the discipline and agility to win in the international races.

Had they used their time and energies on the normal things, they would have run a normal, if not mediocre, life. Had they used their talents to impress their peers, they'd have remained in that class and never interacted with buddies better than them. Had someone like Artur Shah never started out with a mattress shop, He'd never have owned one of the biggest retail chains in East Africa. He'd probably be waiting for a miracle to happen for him to have a large outlay so he could start his first supermarket, even today. The only difference between him and you, is that he humbled himself enough to accept his position them and start off with Nakuru Mattresses. Many multi-nationals started out this way, from a humble beginning to what they are now.

Like them, refuse to use your resources in the normal way. Like them, refuse to use your political voice in the fast-food kiosk. Like them, refuse to use your now-small business muscle n the mundane. Don't sleep on that idea, don't let it collect dust while you wait for world bank to perform the next miracle. Don't expect to run when you are not practicing with trotting.

Don't wait to produce the next block buster if you don't have the cash; you could start at YouTube and climb higher as you learn. Don't wait for a glorious ending if you have not yet started. Don't despise your humble beginning. It's better than never having a start. If you are confused where to start, why not here. why not start by changing your mindset.

Why not start by doing what you can do without selling an arm? It's wonderful to have great dreams, but without executing them they are as good as dead, so start from the humble beginning you have.

What is the speed of a race car as it flags off? The answer is ZERO. Take any moving object as an example; a plane, a rocket, a ship, a kite, a little boy, a jet. They all start at the least speed of 0 and accelerate, some gradually some rapidly, till they reach their maximum speed. That speed car you saw at a speed of more than 300kph, there was a time, still on this journey, when it was travelling at a speed of 10. But it was still travelling, alright?

The driver of the said car was still in high hopes of winning the race, because his car was on the move and gaining speed. What if he'd decided not to take off after flagg-off, waiting for his car to suddenly spring off at 500kph and somehow find himself at the finish line? Sounds outrageous? That's how we appear to life when we sit around waiting for a big leap when we could start from the humble beginnings we have and slowly gain speed and momentum.

My friend if you are in the small leagues, accept that as the truth and play in your league. There was a time when Beckham was paying for an unknown school team, junior school at that. He dreamt of playing in an international team but here he was, he knew he could only be there at that time. he played in the positions that could accommodate him till the bigger positions noticed and accommodated him.

There was a time when Sylvester Stallone was doing extras in movies, and very few at that. He didn't wait till the big guys could give him a major position but kept at it till he made a big position for himself. He developed his muscle in film till he could tackle the industry. Talent was the only recourse he had and he did a good job of exploiting it to success.

Like those who have succeeded before, exploit your recourses in the league they are suited, developing your muscles by and by, failing your way towards success, till you reach the greatest level of greatness. Start with what you have, however meagre, and build on it like a house, which mushrooms from a bare piece of land through a sunken foundation, supported by scaffolds till it becomes the most breathtaking skyscraper in town. if you have a dream, quit dreaming anymore, start implementing it. It's good that you are thinking big, kudos; now is time for action, start simple!

Get as Much Help

Asking for help is not a sign of weakness. It's one of the bravest things you can do. And it can save your life- Lily Collins

There are saints every day. They stand up and help others and live for others and do things for others- Theodore

Get as Much Help

There are two groups of people who will never make it in life: One group think they are self-sufficient in a way that they don't need input from others to succeed. The other group thinks that they can only rely on others to achieve even the slightest step I life. It's hard to discuss which group is worse but both are destined for doom. If you want to achieve greatness in life, these two groups are extreme; Don't fit yourself into any of them.

It is important to note that only God succeeded without ever consulting anyone, because He is perfect in knowledge and power. The rest of us have all sorts of imperfections by our design. Though we may want to visualize ourselves as the masters in our game, there are still other areas that require a bit of working on. Despite our training and experience, things like technological advancement and demographical change will always bring about gaps that need to be filled.

This is where others come in. The greatest inventions were made because someone was brave enough to ask for someone else's help/ input. The biggest zillion dollar establishments were born of investors who put together a team to enable their success. They realized there was a gap in the plan that could be plugged by another person. They noticed a missing skillset that someone else had. They realized a weakness where they could do with a little support.

Drawing from the example of Zuckerberg might seem like a far-fetched idea, considering your outlay as compared to yours. But the principle is still the same. the same way his multi-billion-dollar firm will require a strategic manager, accountants, marketing reps, and even cleaners, your project, however big or small, needs input from outside of yourself.

You can take a little of learning form other's successes and failures. You can do with a little advice. you can do with a little physical help. words of encouragement or even a few more dollars. get as much as you can.

There's an old proverb in my language that goes,"Andu nio indo", loosely translating to, " people are wealth". Don't hesitate to tap into this wealth when you can. One of the reasons why people don't ask for help so easily is fear. They fear someone might make fun of them. They fear that someone will refuse them that much needed help or even consider them inferior. Why would you not fear failing for not asking for help?

People have been laughing at you for living an ordinary life despite your talents and endowments, what difference do you think it would make if they made fun of you for asking for a little help to stardom? Your kindergarten teacher never talks about it yet they helped you with the alphabet, with the loo, with blowing your nose.

I remember my first week in nursery school, which was not an easy one. I had on a pair of closely fitting khaki shorts with an equally fitting button. The problem was compounded by the fact that I had a running stomach by day. Like the bright student I was I would ask for permission to out every time I felt the urge.

Trouble came in the latrine when in my hurried frenzy I would try to undo my pants to no avail. The outfit was so new that ripping it off was out of the question. I'd end up spoiling my shorts, shuffling back to class to report the 'accident', where the teacher would discharge me to go home, houseflies I my wake.

This continued for the second day after that, and the third. I knew my classmates were being polite enough not to laugh in my face, but they were behind my back. On the fourth day I still had a running stomach ad it was not long before I went to the teacher's desk and she gave me permission, as usual. I remained there, looking at her with pitiful eyes.

I had already asked for permission in thoroughly practiced English and that was the end of my vocabulary then so when she regarded me quizzically, I whispered in mother tongue, "Ndwara, mwarimu!" (Please Take me there, teacher). She gave me a motherly smile, instructed the class to recite the ABCDE chart and escorted me to the loo. With the teacher's help. I didn't spoil my pants and remained in class the rest of the day. Those who were waiting for me to turn out to be a dumb head were surprised when I came out on top of the class that term, and the next, and the next.

I imagine how silly I looked, even to the villagers as I walked home stinking bad, with that smelly demi-solid slipping down my feet. I imagine how mum felt as she cleaned me up. How dad felt about his wife's son who could not get his pants down to relieve himself (By the way a son who does not measure up to certain standards belongs to the mother or he must be so has good at something then the father can say, "this is my son". People had marked me as a public liability until I asked for help. That help made me a better person.

Maybe that's how people are taking you right now; a public liability. A wasted recourse. Don't sir on it. Exploit it. It's cool you have a great idea, are super talented, have an under-exploited resource. Tell trusted friend about it. Ask an expert. Get I to a forum. Get those new ideas, after all, new ideas never hurt. If someone can help with their muscles, let them do. If someone else can help with a skill or a tool, get them to help you. A little help will better your best.

You don't necessarily ask for help from people because they are better tan you. You get then to help coz you are better with them. Had God intended for every man to live independent of others, He'd have created each one of us with all the resources at their disposal. them life would have become very boring. But it is not how the world is.

We are all interdependent. We all need teacher Jane to help with our new pair of shorts, not to mention our life's broken pencils, our alphabets, or kerchiefs.... Teacher Jane in turn needs our fees, our attention and structural support from the school of life and the school of life requires a lesson from the community.

That said, the need for help from outside yourself should not be misinterpreted as inability to inability to take positive steps one yourself. People are only there to fulfil a particular purpose in your life and past that they are irrelevant to your success.

Like a construction, someone maybe the plumber, transporter, a simple tool loke a trowel, an input like timber or sand, a consultant, anything else nut you are the construction site, architect and developer. You must be there in the first place.

You must make the decision to develop the property that you are, to something amazing. It is your responsibility as the architect to design what you want to be, and as the developer to source for all other resources to actualize your dreams.

Don't fall for the fallacy that people can make you great. They can't. Keep them close though, for they are tools, materials and implements for you to use. Don't over rely on them. After all, you can use a different set of tools for the same job.

Be Ready For Success

Success is where preparation and opportunity meet- Dobby Unser.

Be Ready For Success

Success may mean different things to different people in different situations. It therefore follows that only you can tell when you have succeeded. To a little boy, learning how to ride a bicycle is a great achievement. Being able to stop an addiction may be success to someone else. Knowing how to prepare a certain dish may be success to another. Having some money left aside in your budget could be your definition of success. Only you can solidly define your goals.

If you thought that achieving a certain goal is the problem, you might be in for a shock when you finally succeed and you don't know what to do with that achievement. You have succeeded in setting up an emergency fund, hacking that addiction, securing a job, building a house ...... So, what now?

That achievement, if unchecked, might have a negative impact in your future and/ or it could plunge you into deeper problem. Instead of building up into a more contented and happier future, a single success can turn out to be a source of tears and agony.

One of the locals in my village once succeeded in leasing his piece of land to a road construction company. This was a large patch of his farm that had been unproductive over the years, with no crop doing well over that area. He had tried all ways possible to make that piece of land fertile but the murram could not support plant growth. He'd tried to sell that unproductive piece of land, even through brokers, to no avail. He'd given up on that useless piece of land until a road nearby went under construction, and eventually the contracting company struck a deal with him, to mine for murram on his farm.

We all knew he'd finally made it in life. Money didn't just flow into his accounts, it flooded. He'd finally succeeded with his murram patch and we envied him. The problem was that he was not prepared for it. Yes, he was prepared to let go of an unproductive piece of land. He was prepared to sell something useless to him, but he was not prepared for the money.

It is natural that he didn't know what to do with the money. Having millions in his accounts required him to make decisions he was not used to. Having that resource meant he had something at his disposal that he was not mentally equipped to utilize.

So, what do you do with more than plural millions in your bank account? Buy land is the first step. Our friend hurriedly bought land, chipped in some building materials and sketched a plan for a house. That's a wise man. Wise until the builders got on site. These are our friend's friends and they know he has more than enough money. Because he's a good man, he brings a crate of beer on-site on the ground-levelling day. They'll be taking beer instead of water. By noon they are too drunk to work, so he takes them to a club where they drink late into the night.

The next day they report to work late with a hangover and an unpaid day. To kill the hangover, he brings them a crate of beer and rushes back to the club to enjoy himself with the barmaid and some other friends. This is the beginning of a pattern.

In a week, the workers complete ground-levelling, as opposed to two days. He pays the builders and gives them a bonus of ksh1000 each. To celebrate the first milestone in his house project, he spoils them with excessive booze over the weekend. The following week a foundation the builders lay the foundation and a slap a slab on top. By now our friend has realized how sweet a lady is, sandwiched in booze and grilled meat.

It comes as a relief to him when the 'engineer' advises him that his slab needs 21 days to bond. He sees this as an opportunity to impress a sumptuous and delicious-looking lady who's proving hard to bed. He has money so he can take her to Zanzibar, which he does. On the 19th day he comes back home with an oversexed girl and a deflated bank account. But he still has some money left which, if managed well, could finish his construction project and leave him some change to start a business. and he knows it.

But Cynthia feels betrayed that "the man of her dreams" went ton vacation with someone else instead of herself. To appease her, her hauls her into a plane and takes her to Mombasa for a couple of days. On his return home, our friend is dead serious and rounds up his builders and resumes work without booze. But his friends are too thirsty and grilled meat with a delicious lady just got sweeter. He resorts to sneaking to a nearby town with Cynthia for their escapades while the builders do their job. The hardware guy has not requested money for his goods, but the numbers are building up.

By close of day on pay-day the builders have not done much, demoralized by the lack of booze a is the tradition in this site, coupled with the fact that there's no supervision around. But we must pay them alongside the hardware guy. Our friend is left with a few thousand shillings, with which, as a wise man who knows what a little money can or not do, he decides to refurbish his old house. This mean the construction has officially stalled.

Well, many do. After a month he falls sick, goes to the hospital and is diagnosed with HIV/AIDS. To avoid shame, our friend commits suicide, and Cynthia takes over his property.

Some have said that money killed him, but I know it is lack of preparedness that did. He was furtively trying to change things but did not have a plan for when things did change. He was selling a piece of land without a plan for money. It is understandable that when he got money without a plan, his life shattered without a plan. He failed to see past the accomplishment, and the accomplishment became his downfall.

This is a common phenomenon in our lives. We struggle so much to accomplish something, but when we do, we don't know what to do next. We find ourselves stranded in the middle of somewhere that could have been great were it not for the lack of a plan. Yes, you really wanted to achieve that goal, but did you ever envision yourself having achieved it?

To enable us put this into perspective, let's consider a football match. In the big leagues the team will always have a plan to score. The players will do all they can to score, employing all their brain and talent till they have achieved their objective. One thing they don't do is get stuck on that one goal. They may celebrate for some time then go back to the pitch and play with the same vigour, even more.

A player can't just go home to celebrate simply because they have scored for their team. They remain in the pitch, playing till the game is over. They already had a plan, as a team, fer what to do after scoring that one goal. It could be to score another goal, or to start playing defensive game henceforth.

A little victory should not stop you from pressing further. instead, it should be the motivation to go on further. But how can you draw from your achievements if you have not planned for them? You need to have milestones, not for the purpose of knowing if you are in the right track, but to keep you going. It's good to celebrate but you don't to celebrate one achievement over and over till you have run out of time and energy. That is a single step you took towards the greater goal.

Though a great journey starts with a single step, you must realize that a journey is made up of many steps. After reaching a certain you may want to stop, heave a sigh, look back and say, "I've come so far" but always remember to resume the journey. Always have a milestone after the milestone to keep you going, else you'll find yourself lost in the maze of life. Always know you'll do what when you succeed in the present undertaking. That helps you to be prepared and to remain focused, it helps you know your way around those small achievements that ultimately make up success.

The adage that it takes numerous battles to win a war holds true. You must fight, win, go back and fight some more, win or win, go back and fight again till you have won the whole war. Don't let the small victory in a single battle, however important it is to you, deceive you into letting your guard down. Know that the war is not yet over. You need to brace yourself for the next battle or simply concede, even after a win in a battle. You need to have a plan, even before the war has started. It could be something like, "if I succeed in securing the frontier, I'll try to locate the infantry and bring it under my control. If I succeed, I'll......" These are very important battles that have their successes but they are only important and meaningful if they build up to a larger goal.

We are not all military men. We all have different dreams and aspirations. The point is to have a plan for when lady luck comes knocking at the door. Will you have a fully fledged freak out or will you open the door wide with a smile and say, "Hey I have been waiting for you. Come let's do this or that"? Show luck, achievement or whatever name you attribute to it that you were expecting them.

Let those good things in life never find you unprepared so that you don't know what to do with them. Some people advocate for expecting the best and planning for the worst. Don't fall into the trap. expect the best and plan for it, while having stops for the worst. Don't let the best things that life could bring your way become your worst nightmare. They might become one, if you are not prepared for them.

Embrace the best things at the door and lead them to a Livingroom you already have prepared for them. Otherwise, success will flee from you if you can't show achievement some hospitality. Don't let the best come to you as a shocker, coz that's one of the worst things that could happen to you.

Be prepared for when you'll win that green card, when you'll be elected, when you'll make it through college, when you bag that money, when you finally beat that addiction. You have succeeded in this one, so what now. Have another milestone waiting, so your life will flow smoothly towards a greater you. Be prepared for success, and plan beyond it.

Set Your Eyes on the Bigger Game

Set Your Eyes on the Bigger Game

Ever wondered why the riche get richer, the poor get poorer and the middle class just struggle to retain their stature? The cause is not the government policies, the economy or some other anterior driving force. the root cause is the person/ individual and the world that he's created around himself, in his mind. The low-income earners believe the rich are so because they were born rich.

By so doing they lock themselves out of ever becoming rich. After all they were unlucky to be born in a poor background, so how can they ever beat that? Using this theory, I reckon, a poor man would need to be physically born again in a rich family for him to become rich.

Perhaps the middle class have a theory, by which they limit themselves, or which they use as a mirror to view themselves. The point is everyone thinks they are the way they are because of some outside force that is beyond their control. "I can't measure up to Alex coz his family owned half this city even before I was born." I can't be like Alice because her dad had a future to extend to her once she did her O levels." Blah blah blah. Am not as learned as Nick but I own a car, which he doesn't; that's great success, isn't it?

The problem with this line of thinking is that it is putting you on a leash. You have pegged yourself o a leash because of someone else, who might have put themselves on a leash too, pegging themselves on someone else. Who said that gut across the street is a standard of measure?

Why would you adjust your pace to fit his speed while you are not running in the same race, not even on the same track? Why would you adjust his thinking to fit his? Because he's someone above you on some ladder, why don't you want to climb yours?

In life, we all have our different and diverse destinies. The good thing is that each destiny is independent of the other despite our familial, social and economic relationships. We are together because we need each other as tools and implements to a cause but we don't determine each other's lives.

Your parents will not determine your life unless you let them, and/or make them the greatest factor in your equation. Your business partner will not determine your financial success unless you make them your business. Your spouse will not determine your success in life unless you make your life all about them. You have a life to live and they have theirs. Don't gauge yourself against them.

It's good that someone complemented you on some achievement. It's okay that you beat someone to a given task/goal. It's okay you don't measure up to someone. The fact is, others have been there, achieved and got their share of glory, looked down upon by those above them, beat someone to a more daunting task and still died unhappy.

They didn't realize the secret to all this: Life was never meant to be a competition. You just live it, love it and make a mark o the globe. If for once you can stop viewing life as a competition, then you can stop measuring yourself against others. The inability of others will stop making you gloat I false glory. others family status and endowments will not put you down, after all you are not running the same race.

One thing about the race of life is that you keep going till it's over. there's no definite number of laps you should do, or even a set time. You can't just quit going coz you have an edge over the rest; once you have an edge over yourself, then, maybe, you can stop. This is simply because you only have yourself to compare with.

You can borrow notes from others but really, it's only you and your life. People have tried in this endeavour and failed, but they are not you. Succeed in it. Everyone in your lineage, from your great grandfather, have lived from hand to mouth but thy are not you; you can live in affluence. Zuckerberg's children were born in a rich family, but that doesn't affect who you are inside. you too can become stinking rich, and bear some rich kids.

What I mean is, you can beat that defeatist attitude and rise high above those limitations. Break lose from the leash, explore more ground. Stop looking at those around you and climb higher than you ever thought. Be creative. You are not limited to the resources at your disposal but by your own mindset.

It's not your level your education that matters, it's your paradigm. It's not ow rich your dad or mum is, it's how rich your mind is. It's not about how many connections you have, how many people you know that know people, it's how connected your mind is. It's not about the material wealth at your disposal, but the wealth of ideas you want to put into practice. Open yourself to success and succeed.

Remove your eyes from what you don't have today and focus o your goal. Stop glancing at the tangents who are people around you and look squarely at he tasks in hand. find ways to do what matters to you most, your goal. Many have bee hare and succeeded because they set their eyes on the bigger game, why not you? You are not meant tor the bin, you are meant for the high table.

Stop trashing yourself while you can do great things. you just need to trust yourself and take one step at a time, eventually you will find yourself there. Remember, if you aim for the sun, you will get to it, why stop at the moon anyway. Have big dreams and don't doubt your sanity when they seem too large. Dream as big as you can, and do as much as you dream.

There's room for Improvement

The biggest room in the world is room for improvement-Helmut Schidt

There's room for Improvement

I used to read it in my school reports and it always sounded like bad news to me. Now I know better; However well or badly you are doing, there's always room for improvement. You can do good, if you were doing badly. You can do better than the good you just did. Your relationship can do better. Your business can perform better. Your grades can improve by some degree, you can write better stuff, sing better ......

There are those who have been held-up inn a loop of frustration. Maybe you are in that group. Everything you put your hand to has been a frustration. You started a project and it didn't quite work well, have been working on a failing relationship for some time, been struggling with an addiction ......

All in all, you haven't hit a pre-defined standard in-so-far. The natural reaction to all this is to give up and brand yourself a failure. The other thing you can do is to condition yourself and your response to those negative outcomes, build on them and succeed.

In primary school, I had a teacher who always taught us to take any experience as a learning experience. We hated the teacher for caning us if we as much as thought something is hard, or it's a problem. To him, every daunting task was a challenge that you had to overcome.

Maths was not hard; it was a challenge for those who didn't see it as fun with numbers. Waking up early in the morning and being in school was not a problem. It was a challenge with time management. Now I understand him, more than then. It's next to impossible to solve a problem as opposed to tackling a challenge.

Through those challenges in life we can learn and gain more insightful information. if you can look at the huddles in life and see learning experiences/ opportunities, you'll enjoy life even more. After all, life is more beautiful because of them. Success won't be success if it had to come on a silver platter.

Did you expect your dreams and expectations to just happen to you? NO! You must try out different ways and methods until you find one that works. If one approach to a challenge doesn't work, well, you now know one way that doesn't work. You didn't fail, you just got an opportunity to learn more methods. Not that you are not smart enough, you just need to pinpoint the missing bit to fix the jigsaw.

Life is not all about touching everything and it becomes gold; most of the time you must work with what you must gain what you don't have. But we are all guilty of being conservative about putting our resources to use. There are so many 'what-ifs' that the most readily available answer is not to act. By not pressing on we fail to apply on very crucial condition, "What if success is just around the corner?" In the book Men of Men, Wilbur Smith has one character, Zougga Ballantine, who sold his quarry claim simply because he had 'hit the blue'.

The blue was a notably hard rock that broke men's backs and their tools. Ballantine had had his share of triumphs with the claim, having retrieved small to medium chunks of diamond, but when his men encountered the blue, he opted to quit mining. To him, the blue was doom to his mining business, an impenetrable end to a mining shaft. To continue employing men on an impregnable rock was a total loss and wastage of resources. But as the story goes, the blue turned out to be the most pure and precious form of diamond.

Fancy that! Ballantine had employed men on a claim that was barely breaking even and sustained his faith until a time when he was just scrapping the surface o f the most precious diamond. Instead of learning something new about diamond, he chickened out.

Ballantine could have done better than to give up. He could have done better than to be contented with his meagre collections, or the paltry sale of an unperforming claim. He could have done better than turn his back on success. He could have asked himself, "What if the blue can serve a better purpose, what if there was a better way to extract the blue from the shaft?" Now you know better.

Don't make the same mistake as Major Ballantine. Don't turn your back on success. Don't sell out when it's breaking your back. There's nothing wrong with you, your undertaking or your plan. It just needs some improvement. Learn from it and give it a better shot.

Like Ballantine, life has been giving you little pieces of diamond, enough to keep you afloat. You may be tempted to be contented with your normal life coz, after all, you are paying your bills, living under a roof and dressing just fine. Under those circumstances you are reluctant even, to agitate the waters. These lilliputian provisions in life are he ones that trick us into accept mediocre life despite our in-built and inborn abilities to do great things. After all you are assured of a great meal before bed.

The underlying question in the mind of a person with a full stomach is, "What if trying this today will deny me the utility of a full stomach tomorrow?" It's man's instinct. You need to outgrow that mindset and start thinking of how to improve your life.

Those before us were just fine wearing animal hides but fine was not very comfortable. By and by they invented and improved textile. Today it's not a question of covering our nakedness but style and fashion, and there's still room for improvement in the textile industry. Don't settle for a business that's just covering your bills.

There's room for improvement. Don't just settle for a relationship that barely covers your bed at the expense of your happiness. don't settle for anything common, you have everything it takes to do better. You just need to think without a box.

Discard those notions that you can only reach a certain level. Those achievements are nothing compared to the broader scope of success in life. Celebrate them, hang them as souvenirs on the wall, then go back to the field and better your best. Success in life is made up of many achievements and learning experiences in the guise of failures.

Apply those skill-sets you learn from the school of life to attain a certain goal and once you have succeeded in something, gather some more insight and work some more to make it shine. This way you can, and will, eventually rise to stardom, one step at a time.

You don't want to sit on a single achievement, or lack thereof, and slowly become irrelevant in your life and the lives of others. Instead, keep on chipping till you have sculpted the success you have ever dreamt of and even then, there'll always be room for improvement.

Don't miss out!

Visit the website below and you can sign up to receive emails whenever Lawrence Muigai publishes a new book. There's no charge and no obligation.

https://books2read.com/r/B-A-OEDKB-XEBHD

BOOKS 2 READ

Connecting independent readers to independent writers.

Also by Lawrence Muigai

Wisdom of the Sower

www.ingramcontent.com/pod-product-compliance
Lightning Source LLC
Chambersburg PA
CBHW061403160726

47995CB00001B/434